Truth, Tales and Visions:

Rabbi Nachman of Breslov's Wisdom

EDITED AND TRANSLATED BY
YAACOV DAVID SHULMAN

Dot-Letter-Word Books

ISBN: 9798793604826

CONTENTS

INTRODUCTION

Rabbi Nachman of Breslov (1772-1810), great-grandson of the founder of Hasidism, the Baal Shem Tov (1700-1760), was himself a pivotal figure in the process of Jewish spirituality. The Baal Shem Tov taught a heart-felt path of Torah based on an inclusive love of all Jews. His teachings stressed the ability of all Jews to serve God in joy, and the new customs of Hasidism provided a means for Jews to feel a camaraderie with each other and a connection to tzaddikim, spiritual masters.

Rabbi Nachman did not attempt to organize the Baal Shem Tov's teachings; rather, he attempted to take them to the next level. He was a man of passions and simple striving to serve God; he was a man of poetry and imagination; a man of holiness and holy longing; a man of feeling, a man of titanic inner struggles, a man of impulse, brutal honesty, deep love, a man who was forever struggling, growing, joyous, suffering, human and holy. Rabbi Nachman's teachings reached out, awakened the flame within a person's heart to race toward God. And then Rabbi Nachman's techniques of serving God gave a person the tools with which to channel that fiery enthusiasm: for instance, the stress on joy, on broad and all-inclusive learning without intellectual self-doubt, and, perhaps most of all, the championing of hitbodedut, lone, spontaneous prayer to God.

Rabbi Nachman transmitted his teachings not only in conventional ways, but also related tales, dreams, visions and parables.

Rabbi Nachman's teachings have a particular appeal to the artistic, creative individual. Rabbi Nachman was himself a poetic and idiosyncratic personality whose spirit expressed itself in a number of ways. From his childhood, he loved to roam in the forests and fields alone, communing with God, and he later institutionalized this as the system of spontaneous prayer called hitbodedut. He reported dreams and visions and told brilliant allegorical tales that are supreme examples of the imagination deeply integrated with mystical consciousness.

His teachings are often poetic and playfully associative. His startling leaps of intuition, connecting apparently unrelated topics, are expressions of "non-linear, right-brain" thinking.

Rabbi Nachman appears as one of the first teachers of popular psychology. His teachings stress self-esteem, simple striving, self-application. Yet they are simultaneously not simple at all. Rabbi Nachman's teachings are a combination of the simple and the opaque, of Torah for the tzaddik and Torah for the most simple person.

His teachings may appear to be marvelously simple and inspiring. But the simplicity is a mask for something deeper. Rabbi Nachman said that neither his adversaries nor his followers understood who he is. Rabbi Nachman remains mysterious forever. He is accessible and inaccessible.

He says something that we seem to understand, yet when we examine it, it seems to have shifted, to have turned about. We define him, yet he will not stay defined. No label ever covers him.

Rabbi Nachman lived a life that he compared to the moon, a life of constant struggle and spiritual growth, closeness and distance. So does a person who connects to the path of Rabbi Nachman feel that he also must constantly struggle and grow, sometimes distant but sometimes very close.

1. FAITH AND HOPE

Great Things

People say that one doesn't have to look for great things. But I say that one has to search only for great things.

Without Eating or Drinking

This world contains wisdom so great that one could live on it and not require food or drink.

Believe in Yourself

If you are small in faith, you will find it difficult to serve God.
You must have faith that God loves you and considers you important.

Find the Hidden Good

Judge everyone favorably. Search for even a little bit of goodness. In that little bit of goodness, that person isn't bad.

When you do this, you can raise someone from guilt to merit. You can bring him to repentance.

Even if someone is bad, how is it possible that he doesn't have at least a little bit of good? How could it be that he never did something good?

Apply this to yourself as well.

Even if you see that you are full of wrong-doing, search for some little bit of good.

Maybe your good deed was flawed and filled with ulterior motives. But how is it possible that it didn't contain some bit of good?

Find that little bit of good and rejoice.

Search again and find more goodness.

Gather all the good points.

When you do this, you make spiritual melodies with your soul. You are like a musician plucking the notes of a melody.

A Spirit of Folly

Where do sins come from? They come from a lack of understanding. "A man does not sin unless a spirit of folly has entered into him" (Sotah 3a).

This is the greatest pity of all. Have compassion on those who have sinned; fill them with understanding.

Bring Forth Goodness

Be good and serve God honestly. Do this constantly. The good will remain, and the bad will fall away of itself.

Expertise On All Levels

Even if you fall to the depths of hell, do not despair. Constantly search for God. Strengthen yourself in any way you can, for God is even found in hell. There too you can cling to Him. "If I spread out my couch in Sheol, You are there" (Psalms).

Do Not Despair

Even if you have fallen very low, do not despair. There is no despair in the world. "Sins can be turned into merits" (Yoma 86b). This matter contains mystical secrets.

You can easily return to God from any fall, because God's greatness has no end. Never give up crying out to God.

All Who Hope

"Be strong and mighty, all who hope for God" (Psalms 31:25). Even if you have not reached any level of holiness but you only hope, still, "be strong and mighty." Do not let anything upset you.

If You Believe That You Can Break...

If you believe that you can break, believe that you can fix.

The Dance

"How does one dance before the bride?"
How can you dance beyond your present level?

A Broken Heart

Here is a sign that you have attained a broken heart:

Even while you stand among others, you can turn your face aside and call out to God.

The Cry from the Heart

The cry from the heart is itself faith.

Even if you have many doubts, when you cry out, your heart still has a spark of holy faith. If not, you would not have cried out.

This faith is still very small. By crying out, you can enlarge your faith until your questions fall away. But even if you do not reach that level, crying out is still very good.

Self-Renewal

Always strengthen yourself and begin anew, as though you are starting for the very first time.

Even if you are falling, be strong in your intent to come close to God. Yearn for Him, cry out to Him, pray—do whatever you can to serve Him with joy.

A Dream

Rabbi Nachman told:

I dreamed that I was sitting in my room. No one came to see me, and I was very surprised. I went to the other room, but there was no one there either. I went into the house and then into the study hall, but there was no one there.

I decided to go out. I saw people standing in circles, whispering. One made fun of me, another laughed at me, another looked at me arrogantly. Even my followers were against me. A few acted insolently, a few whispered secretly about me, and the like.

I called one of my followers over and asked him, "What is going on?"

He replied, "How could you have done such a thing? Is it possible that you committed such a great sin?"

I had no idea why they were mocking me. I asked him to bring together all my followers. He left me, and I didn't see him again.

I sat alone, trying to decide what to do. Finally, I decided to travel to another country.

But when I got there, people were standing about and speaking about this. Even there, they knew about it.

I decided to go live in a forest. Five of my followers joined me, and together we went to the forest. We lived there, and whenever we needed anything, such as food and the like, one of them would go and buy it. I would always ask him if the commotion had died down, and he would always say, "No, is still very strong."

While we were living there, an old man came and called me. He said that he had something to talk about with me.

I went with him, and he began to speak with me.

He said, "Did you really do such a thing? How can you not be ashamed before your grandfather, Rabbi Nachman, and before your great-grandfather, the Baal Shem Tov? How can you not be ashamed before the Torah of Moses and before our holy forefathers, Abraham, Isaac and Jacob, and the others? Do you think that you will live here forever? Won't your money run out? And you are a weak person. What will you do?

"Do you think that you will go to another country? What good will it do? If they don't know who you are, you won't be able to stay there because they won't give you any money. And if they do know who you are, you won't be able to live there because they will know about this."

I answered him, "Since this is so and I must keep running, at least I have the world-to-come."

He replied, "Do you think you have the world-to-come? You committed such a desecration of God's name that you won't even have a place to hide in Gehennom."

I said, "Go away. I thought that you would comfort me, but you are making me suffer. Go away."

The old man left me.

As I sat there, I decided that since I am staying here for such a long time, I may forget all of my learning. I told one of the men that when he went to the city he should look for a book and bring it back with him.

He went to the city but he returned without a book. He said that it was impossible. He could not tell whom the book was for, of course; and it was impossible to take it secretly.

I suffered very much: first, because I was wandering about, and now, because I didn't have a book and I might forget my learning entirely.

A while later, the old man returned, carrying a book under his arm.

I asked him, "What are you carrying?"

"A book."

"Give it to me."

He gave me the book. When I took it, I didn't even know how to hold it. And when I opened it, I didn't have any idea what was in it. It was as though it were in a foreign language and a foreign script. This caused me a great deal of suffering. I was afraid that if my followers found out about this, they would leave me.

The old man again came over to speak with me. I went with him, and he again began to tell me, "How could you have done such a thing? How can you not be ashamed? You won't even have a place to hide in Gehennom."

I told him, "If a man from the upper world would tell me this, I would believe him."

He said, "I am from there"; and he gave me a sign.

I recalled the well-known story of the Baal Shem Tov. The Baal Shem Tov had once thought that he had no portion in the world-to-come, and he said, "I love God without the world-to-come."

I threw my head back with very great bitterness. When I threw my head back, all the people before whom the old man said I should be ashamed came to me: my grandfather, the forefathers, and so forth. They quoted the verse to me, "The fruit of the land will be for glory and beauty" (Isaiah 4:2). They told me, "Now we will take pride in you."

They brought me all my followers and children (because at first even my own children had deserted me), and they consoled me.

As for how I threw my head back—even if a person had sinned eight hundred times against the entire Torah, if he were to throw his head back with such bitterness, he would certainly be forgiven.

As for the rest of the good, I do not want to tell you. But it was certainly good.

2. COMING CLOSE TO GOD

Simplicity

The essence of serving God is simplicity: in learning a great deal, praying a great deal and doing good deeds.

You do not have to be too strict with yourself. The Torah was not given to angels.

Simply do what you can.

Fanaticism

It isn't necessary to be a fanatic.

When someone casts aside all the concerns of this world and only serves God, people call him a fanatic. I myself don't regard such behavior as fanaticism. To the contrary, it is when one runs after this-worldly things and is far from God that one is really a fanatic.

Still, even what the world calls fanaticism is unnecessary. One can be a kosher person without fanaticism.

Step by Step

Serve God at every moment. Learn a great deal; do many good deeds; pray a great deal, pouring out your heart to God.

Don't get overwhelmed. Don't try to do everything at once. Go at a comfortable pace, one step at a time.

If you stumble, remember that "the Compassionate One forgives a person who is under duress" (Bava Kama 28b).

Always yearn for God. This yearning is itself a great thing. As the Talmud states, "The Compassionate One desires the heart."

Desire God

No angel or seraph can boast that it can truly serve God.
But you must always desire to come close to Him.
In the midst of this desire, pray, learn Torah and do good deeds.
You don't need to be clever. You merely need simplicity.
But even in simplicity, don't be a fool.

Receiving the Torah

When the people of Israel received the Torah, they had great wisdom. In their day, there were idol worshippers whose error was a result of great wisdom and philosophy.

If the Jews hadn't cast aside that wisdom, they would not have received the Torah. They would have been able to deny everything, and nothing that Moses did for them would have helped. Not even all the awesome miracles he performed would have helped.

But Israel, being a holy nation, saw the truth. They cast aside their wisdom and "believed in God and Moses His servant." As a result, they received the Torah.

The Crown of the Messiah

In the days before the messiah comes, there will be a flood of skepticism. The highest mountains will be covered, and the waters will even dash over the land of Israel.

They will spray into kosher hearts; and through sophistication, no one will find an answer.

The kingdom will stand only because of simple Jews who recite psalms and serve God simply.

Therefore, when the messiah comes, it is the simple people who will place the crown upon his head.

The Simplicity of God

You do not need cleverness to serve God—just simplicity and faith.

Simplicity is the highest level. God Himself is higher than everything, and He is the ultimately simple being.

The Clever Man and the Simple Man

Once, when the king was going through the census records, he saw the names Clever and Simple.

He was intrigued.

He very much wanted to meet these two people. But it occurred to him that if he summoned them suddenly, they would be very frightened. The clever man wouldn't know what to answer, and the simple man might even go mad.

So the king decided that he would send a clever messenger to the clever man and a simple messenger to the simple man.

He gave each messenger a letter.

He also gave them letters for the governor of the state where the two men lived.

The clever and simple messengers came to the governor, and gave him their letters.

The governor inquired about Clever and Simple.

He was told that Clever was incredibly brilliant and very wealthy. And Simple was very simple, with one rough fur coat that he treated as though it were an entire wardrobe.

The governor decided that it would not be right to bring the simple man to the king in such a coat. He made him good clothing and placed them in the simple messenger's carriage. Then he gave both messengers their letters.

When the simple man received his letter, he told the messenger, "I don't know what the letter says. Read it to me."

The messenger replied, "I can recite it to you by heart. The king wants you to come to him right away."

The simple man asked, "You aren't making fun of me?"

"No, not at all. It's really true."

The simple man was filled with joy. He ran to his wife and told her, "My wife, the king has sent for me."

She asked him, "What's going on? Why does he want you?"

But he had no time to answer. He quickly and joyfully hurried into the carriage to travel with the messenger.

Then, when he saw the clothing, he was even happier than before: on top of everything, he has clothes!

And he was very happy.

Meanwhile, when the clever messenger gave his letter to the clever man, the clever man said, "Wait and stay here overnight. We'll talk and decide what to do."

That night, the clever man invited the messenger for dinner. As they ate, the clever man began thinking aloud, using his intellect and philosophical training: "What can this mean? What kind of king would send for an insignificant person like me? Such a great king who has such a great government! Should I say that he sent for me because of my intelligence? But he must have intelligent people around him, and he himself must be very intelligent. So why should he want me?"

He thought this over a great deal. And finally, he turned to the messenger and said, "Do you know what I think? It's clear that there is no king at all. The whole world has made a mistake thinking that there is a king.

"The whole thing is ridiculous. How could it be that the whole world would let itself be ruled by one man? Obviously, there isn't any king who rules the world."

The clever messenger protested, "But I brought you a letter from the king."

The clever man asked him, "Did you yourself take the letter from the king's hand?"

"No. Someone else delivered the letter to me."

"That proves my point! Examine this closely and you will see that I am right: there is no king."

The clever man asked the messenger further, "Tell me, you grew up in the royal city. Did you ever see the king?"

"No." (And in fact, not everyone gets to see the king, because he only appears on rare occasions.)

"Now you see that I am right and that there is obviously no king. You yourself never even saw him."

The clever messenger asked, "If that's so, who is running the country?"

The clever man replied, "I will tell you—and I am sure about this. I've traveled through many lands. In Italy, seventy men lead the country, each one taking a turn. This same thing must be in this case."

The clever man's words began to persuade the messenger, until they both decided that there is obviously no king in the world.

The Blink of an Eye

Do not put off till tomorrow what you can do today. The world does not stand still for even the blink of an eye.

Do whatever you can in serving God without a moment's delay. Who knows how many obstacles you will have in the future? You have only this moment.

Sometimes, no matter how hard you try, you can't succeed.

Wait without growing discouraged. Wait until your time comes.

As you wait, continue to yearn for God.

Do not despair of anything.

As soon as God helps, do whatever you can with great enthusiasm.

It is Forbidden to Despair

Never despair.

Even if you are on the absolutely lowest level, even if you are in the depths of hell, do not despair. "From the belly of the depths have I called out" (Jonah 2:3). Strengthen yourself with whatever you can. Believe that you can receive life from the Torah.

Strengthen oneself to the greatest extent possible, for there is no despair in the world at all. Even if you have fallen, when you strengthen yourself, you can still hope to return to God.

3. JOY

The Task of Joy

Gather all your resources to be constantly happy.

A broken heart is very good. But that is only for a limited amount of time.

Set aside a block of time every day to break your heart and speak to God in your own words.

But for the rest of the day, be joyful.

Accept Everything with Joy

Even if God were to take my life, I would accept that with great joy.

The Greatness of Faith

The world considers faith a small thing. But I consider faith a very great matter.

The World Was Created for Faith

God foresaw that there would be people who would have problems with their faith; doubts would arise in their minds, but they would struggle and strengthen their faith. Only for this did God create the universe.

4. TORAH

The Chambers of Torah Insight

There are chambers of Torah. Each room has several doors that lead into other rooms.

These rooms are filled with treasures. As one passes through the rooms, one gathers these precious and lovely treasures.

But be careful not to fool yourself. You cannot reach such a level quickly.

Yearning to Learn

It may be that you find it impossible to learn. Yet your heart is on fire to learn Torah and serve God. The very desire to learn is like learning.

Sometimes, two tzaddikim talk with one another. But they are hundreds of miles apart.

One tzaddik asks a question on the Torah, and the other tzaddik says something that answers the question.

Sometimes both tzaddikim ask a question, and the question of one answers the question of the other.

In this way, these two tzaddikim talk with one another. But only God hears them.

God binds their words together.

Then He writes their words in a book.

This book is the spiritual, supernal heart.

When your heart is on fire with the desire to learn Torah, you receive a heart from the supernal heart, the book of remembrance. It was from there that your initial desire to learn originated.

Then it is as though you have actually learned.

When the Torah Shows its Love

When the Torah shows you its love, you won't even desire the world-to-come. You will only want to learn Torah.

Discipline and Liberation

Even people who are very far from holiness, people who have become habitual sinners, can be inspired by Torah learning to abandon their conduct. If they will take on a strict schedule of a certain amount of learning per day, they will free themselves.

The power of Torah is immense.

Dozing Off While Learning

Even learning Torah while dozing off is good.

Learn Aloud

When learning Torah, speak the ideas aloud in your own words. This is good for the world.

The Traveler through Torah

Go through all of the Torah.

The great princes tour various countries and spend vast sums of money so that they will be able to boast about all the places that they visited.

Visit all areas of the Torah. When you arrive at the world-to-come, you will be able to boast that you were everywhere. Then you will recall everything you learned.

How to Learn Torah

Learn simply and fast. Do not confuse yourself by comparing what you are learning now with what you learned before.

At times, you may not understand something. Don't spend too much time worrying about it. Let it go and continue learning.

You will learn a great deal and come to review the texts several times. The second or third time, you will understand whatever you didn't grasp at first.

And if you still don't understand some points, what of it? You will have more than made up for that by your vast amount of learning.

Success through Visualization

If your intent to learn Torah is very strong, what you visualize will come to pass.

For instance, you may visualize that you will learn the entire Shulchan Aruch with its major commentaries. Visualize how you will learn and in how much time—for instance, learn five pages a day, finishing within a year. You must visualize this so strongly that your imagination is bound up in it. Desire it strongly and think about it deeply. As a result, you will successfully carry out your intentions.

God Enjoys Your Torah Thoughts

When creating original Torah thoughts, believe in yourself. Believe that God derives a great deal of pleasure from your thoughts. Keep creating new insights and write them down until you produce entire books.

As a result, all strict judgments will be ameliorated.

Creating Rivers of Torah

When you create Torah thoughts, a spring begins to flow.

A spring is at first small and narrow. Afterwards it grows deeper and broader until rivers flow, and everyone comes to drink from those waters.

Creating One's Own Torah Thoughts

Creating original Torah thoughts is a great rectification for thoughts of sin.

Sinful thoughts are a result of the power of imagination.

When you use your imagination to delve into the holy Torah, you rectify it.

Torah Insights

New Torah insights are on the level of the Messiah.

Giving God Joy

When you create Torah insights, you give God joy.

Cultivating Torah Insights

When creating Torah thoughts, mentally repeat the verse or topic that you are studying; pray until the door of understanding is opened.

At times, a thought may flash through your mind. You must have a great deal of strength to capture it.

The Protection of Learning Jewish Law

Learn Jewish law both before and after creating original Torah thoughts.

Then you are preceded and followed by soldiers. The Torah that you learn can descend into the world and you can walk safely, for the soldiers do not allow evil influences to approach.

Torah Without Insights

It may be that although you are learning Torah, you do not have any original insights. The intelligence of the Torah is still unborn.

Cry out to God. You will bring forth the intelligence of the Torah into the world, like a baby being born.

If you learn Torah but have no original insights, do not teach it to others.

It is true that God delights in it. But still, only teach material that you have made your own.

Clarifying Character through Halachah

When one sins, one mixes good and evil.

By learning Jewish law, which distinguishes between kosher and unkosher, allowed and forbidden, pure and impure, you separate good from evil.

Every day, learn at least one paragraph from the Shulchan Aruch. When you have more time, learn through the four sections of the Shulchan Aruch. After finishing all four sections, go through them again. Do this for the rest of your life.

Guarding One's Mind

Continuously renew your mind.

When you renew your mind, you renew your soul, for the mind and the soul are one.

The Map of Time and Space

There was a king who had an object shaped like a hand.

This hand was the map of all worlds. Everything that existed since heaven and earth were created until the very end and even afterwards was illustrated on that hand. The lines and wrinkles of the hand illustrated in detail the structure of all the worlds, together with everything in each world.

The lines of the hand formed letters. Just as letters are written on a map next to every object to identify it, so were the lines of the hand like letters. The letters stood next to every object and identified it.

Each state, each city, all the rivers, bridges, mountains and everything else were illustrated in the lines and wrinkles of the hand. And next to each object stood letters telling what it was. All the people who lived in each state and everything that they lived through was illustrated on the hand. Even all the roads from one state to the other and from one area to another were there.

The pathway from one world to another was also pictured there.

There is a pathway on which one can go from earth to heaven (people cannot go from earth to heaven because they do not know the way; but there, the pathway by which one can go up to heaven was illustrated). All the pathways that exist between one world and the next were illustrated there.

Elijah went up to heaven on one pathway, and that pathway was illustrated there.

Moses went up to heaven on another pathway, and that pathway was illustrated there.

Enoch went up to heaven on another pathway, and that pathway was illustrated there.

And so from one world to the next world, everything was illustrated in the lines and wrinkles of the hand.

Everything was illustrated as it had existed at the time that the world was created; as it is today; and as it will be in the future. For instance, there was an illustration of Sodom as it had been before it was overturned; an illustration of Sodom being overturned; and an illustration of how Sodom looks today after it was overturned.

Everything was illustrated on the hand: what was, what is and what will be.

5. MELODY

Even if You Cannot Sing Well, Sing

Cheer yourself up by singing.
If you cannot sing well, at least sing when you are alone.
You cannot imagine the worth of a tune.

The Melody of Faith

Every wisdom has its own tune.

The higher a wisdom is, the higher is its tune. Ultimately, you can rise to the beginning of creation, the beginning of emanation. There is nothing higher than that. It is surrounded by nothing but the light of the infinite God, which contains all creation and wisdom.

That level of wisdom cannot be apprehended, for the Infinite One is God Himself, Whose wisdom cannot be understood. Only faith applies there: faith that the Infinite One's light surrounds all universes.

Faith has its own tune.

The tune of faith in the light of the Infinite One is higher than all other tunes.

The tunes of all other faiths are drawn from this tune.

In the future, "The nations will have a clear speech to call together in the name of God" (Zephaniah 3:9). Everyone will believe in God.

The New Song of the Future

In the future, the entire universe will operate on the level of wonders, according to providence and not nature.

Then a new song shall arise. "Sing a new song to God, for He has done wonders" (Psalms 98:1).

This song of the future is a song of God's providence and wonders.

There is also a song of nature: "The heavens tell the glory of God, the work of His hands are proclaimed by the firmament" (Psalms 19:2). This is the praise that is sung to God for the way the world is run now.

But in the future, there will be a song of wonders and providence, for then the world will be ruled by providence alone.

6. STORIES

Stories Wake People Up

People say that stories are good for putting people to sleep. But I say that stories are good for waking people up.

Folk Tales and Holy Secrets

Folk tales contain many secrets and exalted matters. But they have been corrupted. A great deal is missing, and they are confused and not told in the proper order. That which belongs in the beginning is told at the end, and the like.

But they really contain very hidden, exalted matters.

Foolish Things

Constantly make yourself happy, even if you have to do foolish things and make silly jokes.

The Story of the Humble King

Once upon a time, there was a king who had a wise advisor. The king told his advisor, "There is another king whose seal claims that he is very powerful and also a truthful, humble man.

"I know that he is powerful. His country is surrounded by the sea. His navy is armed with cannon and doesn't let anyone pass through. Besides that, large swamps surround the country. Only one small trail passes through them, on which only one man can pass. Cannon are also mounted there. When someone comes to attack, the cannons keep him out.

"But as for his claim that he is a truthful and humble man, I don't know about that.

"So I want you to bring me his portrait."

This king had the portraits of all the kings—with that one exception, because no king had his portrait. He was hidden: he sat behind a curtain, far from his subjects.

The wise man went to that county. He decided that he would have to know the quality of the country—how the country operates. And how could he learn the quality of the country? Through its humor.

When one wants to understand something, one must know the jokes that relate to it.

There are all sorts of jokes. Sometimes, a person means to harm someone else; and when the other person protests, he says, "I was only joking," "like one who shoots firebrands, arrows and deadly weapons, and says, I am merely joking" (Proverbs 26:18-19).

Other times, someone only wants to be funny, but his words hurt someone else.

There are all types of jokes.

There is a country that is the archetype of all countries. This country contains a city that is the archetype of all the cities in the country. That city contains a house that is the archetype of all the houses in the city. In that house is a person who is the archetype of all the houses. That person is busy making all the humor and jokes of the entire country.

The wise man took a great deal of money with him, and went there.

He saw that people were engaged in all kinds of tricks and jokes. He understood that the jokes were filled with falsehood. He saw that when people do business, they cheat each other. When someone files a claim, the court is filled with lies, and the judges take bribes. When one goes to a higher court, it too is filled with lies.

And the people used to make humorous skits of all these things.

The wise man understood from these jokes that the country was full of lies and cheating, and that there was no truth there at all.

He began to engage in business, and let himself be cheated. He filed a claim in the courts. The judges were all full of lies and took bribes.

One day he would give a bribe; the next day the judges would say that they didn't recognize him.

He went to a higher court, and that was also filled with lies. Finally, he came before the supreme court.

The supreme court was also filled with lies and bribery.

At last, he came to the king.

He called out, "Over whom are you a king? From beginning to end, the country is filled with lies. There isn't any truth here at all." He began to describe all the falsehood of the country.

When the king heard this, he bent his ear to the curtain. It was incredible to him that someone should know the falseness of the county. When the ministers heard the wise man, they grew angry. But he continued speaking out and describing the falsehood of the country.

The wise man cried out, "One might say that you are like everyone else, that you also love falsehood. But the opposite is true. You are a man of truth. You are far from the people because you cannot stomach their lies."

He began to praise the king extravagantly.

The king was very humble. "Where his greatness was, there was his humility" (Megillah 31a). This is the way of a humble person: the more he is praised, the more humble does he become in his own eyes.

Since the wise man praised the king so much, the king became extremely humble, until he became absolutely nothing.

He could no longer hold himself back, and he threw aside the curtain. "Who is this man who understands all of this?"

The king's face was revealed. The wise man saw it, painted his portrait and brought it to his king.

AND VISIONS

7. WORTHY LEADERS

The Man of Compassion

A leader must have compassion.

He must know how to handle his compassion. For instance, one may not be compassionate to thieves or murderers. And one must direct one's compassion correctly. One gives a baby milk, and an older person food. One gives each individual what he needs.

Only Moses completely filled this role. He was the leader of Israel in the past, and he will be the leader in the future. "That which was will be" (Ecclesiastes 1:4).

Moses was ready to sacrifice his life without a moment's thought. When God threatened to destroy the Jewish people during the episode of the golden calf, He told Moses, "I will make from you a great nation" (Exodus 32:10). But Moses paid no attention. Instead, he said, "Please forgive their sin" (Ibid. 32).

Moses worked hard to spread civilization: to fill the world with human beings, people with understanding.

He revealed that there is a God Who rules the earth.

The Tzaddik is Both Above and Below

The tzaddik must show a person on the lowest level that he is still close to God. The tzaddik must waken him and tell him, "God is with you; do not be afraid, for He is next to you; 'the entire earth is full of His glory' (Isaiah 6:3)."

Even if you fall to the lowest rung, you can return to God.

Encourage yourself with the fact that you realize how far you are. At first, you didn't even know that. The fact that you know how far you are itself means that you are coming close to Him.

The Light That Shines in a Thousand Universes

There is a light that shines in a thousand universes. This light is so great that a normal person cannot absorb it—only a great, wise person, one who can divide thousands into hundreds. Such a person can divide the great light into smaller portions so that others can absorb it bit by bit.

The Field of Souls

There is a field in which extraordinarily beautiful trees and grasses grow. The beauty of that field cannot be described.

These trees and grasses are holy souls.

But some souls are naked. They wander outside the field, waiting to get rectified so that they can return to their place. Sometimes, even a great soul leaves the field and finds it hard to return.

All of them look to the master of the field.

Whoever desires to be the master of the field must be a powerful warrior, a broad-shouldered man and a very great tzaddik. He must be an extraordinary human being.

Some people can only reach this level with their death. Even to do that, one must be very great. There are many great people who will not reach this level even with their death.

Only a person on an extraordinarily high level can accomplish all that he needs to in his lifetime. He must suffer many troubles and difficult experiences.

And then he can labor in the field. And when he rectifies the souls and brings them back to the field, they can pray.

The master of the field is in charge of constantly watering the trees and tending to the other needs of the field. For instance, he keeps the trees at a proper distance from each other, so that they do not weaken each other.

When the eyes of the master of the field shine, he can look at every individual and see if that individual is close to the ultimate purpose. When someone is distant from that purpose, his prayer is not yet perfect, for he cannot make his entire prayer into a unity. When he finishes saying a word, he has already forgotten its beginning, and he cannot integrate his prayer into oneness.

The master of the field gazes upon him and brings him to the ultimate purpose, which is entirely one.

Mercy, the Heart and the Spring

The true man of mercy is a very great man. I (that is, the stutterer who was telling this story) gather together all true acts of mercy, and I bring them to the true man of mercy.

From them, time is created.

Time exists only as a result of true acts of mercy.

There is a mountain. On the mountain is a stone. From the stone flows a spring.

And everything has a heart. The entire world has a heart. The heart of the world is a complete being, with a face and hands and feet. The toenail of the heart of the world has more heart than any other heart.

The mountain with the spring is at one end of the world. And the heart of the world is at the other end of the world.

The heart stands opposite the spring and constantly longs to come to it. The yearning of the heart for the spring is very deep. The heart constantly calls out that it wants to come to the spring.

And the spring longs for the heart.

The heart has two weaknesses. One is because the sun chases and burns it. The other is because of its constant yearning and longing. It reaches out to the spring and calls out that it wishes to come to the spring. The heart stands opposite the spring and calls out.

It yearns more and more for the spring.

When the heart needs to rest and catch its breath, a great bird comes. It spreads its wings over the heart and shields it from the sun.

Then the heart rests a little.

But even while it is resting, it looks to the spring with yearning.

Since it yearns so much for the spring, why doesn't it go there?

As soon as the heart starts to move to the mountain where the spring is, it no longer sees the top of the mountain, so it can't see the spring. As soon as it doesn't see the spring, it starts to die, for the life force of the heart is drawn only from the spring.

If the heart were to die, the entire world would be destroyed, for the heart is the life-force of everything. And how can the world exist without the heart?

So the heart cannot go to the spring. It stands opposite the spring, longing and crying out constantly that it wishes to come to the spring.

As for the spring, it has no time at all. It is not within the realm of time.

If so, how can the spring be in the world?

The time of the spring comes only because the heart gives the spring a day as a present. When the day comes to an end, the spring will have no time, and it will leave the world.

If the spring no longer exists, the heart will die. Then the entire world will cease to exist.

When the end of the day approaches, the heart and spring begin to part from one another. They begin to tell each other very beautiful parables and poems with great love and longing for each other: the heart for the spring, and the spring for the heart.

The true man of mercy watches over this. Just before the day ends, the true man of mercy comes and gives the heart a day.

The heart gives the day to the spring.

Then the spring once again has time.

When the new day arrives, it brings with it parables and beautiful songs which contain all types of wisdom.

Each day has a different quality. There is Sunday, Monday, and so on. There is also a first day of the month and the holidays.

All the time that the true man of mercy has comes through me, for I (the stutterer) am the one who goes out and gathers together all the true acts of mercy, from which time is created.

The Journey of the Dead Merchant

There was a man from Reisen (White Russia) who had traveled to the land of Israel together with the holy and well-known tzaddik, Rabbi Menachem Mendel of Vitebsk.

It was decided that he would go to collect money for the Jews of the land of Israel, as is the custom.

While he was sailing, he died. Meanwhile, no one in the land of Israel knew of this.

After he died, he imagined that he was traveling to Leipzig with his servant and wagon driver to do business, as he had done during his lifetime, for he had been an important merchant.

On the way, he began to yearn to travel to Rabbi Menachem Mendel.

He wanted to put everything aside and turn back in the middle of the trip. But when he told his men what he intended to do, they began to make fun of him. How could he consider losing business? In this way, they kept him from going to Rabbi Menachem Mendel.

Afterwards, he again had a great desire to go to his rabbi. Again, when he told his men, they dissuaded him. How could such a great merchant turn back from Leipzig and travel to his rabbi's house?

Again, he listened to them.

But afterwards, he again had a burning desire and he declared, "I am not going to listen to you." He wanted very badly to set everything aside and to travel to his rabbi.

The more his men argued with him, the more stubborn he grew, and ordered them to turn around and travel with him.

When they saw that they could not dissuade him, they said that they would no longer listen to him.

He insisted that they do what he says, but they refused.

He grew very angry. He was in charge, he said, and they must do whatever he says.

Then they told him the truth: that he was already dead, and that they were destructive beings who were leading him about and fooling him.

He said, "Now I really insist that you take me to the tzaddik at once."

They said, "Now we really refuse," and they began to argue a legal case with him.

Finally, the case came to the highest court.

The court ruled that they must listen to him and take him immediately.

At once, they brought him to Rabbi Menachem Mendel of Vitebsk, who was still alive and in the land of Israel.

When this man entered the house of the tzaddik, one of the destructive angels entered with him, and the tzaddik was so frightened that he fainted.

After Rabbi Menachem Mendel was revived, he spent about eight days working on this man until he rectified him.

He told the others that the messenger had died, for they still had not learned of it, and he told them the entire story.

How to Become a Tzaddik

Some say that only a person with a very great soul can become a tzaddik.

This is not true. It all depends on one's good deeds, hard work and service of God.

You can come to the highest level. Everything depends on your will. Have mercy on oneself and realize what is really good for you.

Untutored Piety

You can be a kosher person even if you don't know how to learn. You can even be a tzaddik without being a scholar.

The Tzaddik and Trust in God

You can be a tzaddik even if your trust in God isn't perfect.

Vision of the Man in the Circle

I will tell you what I saw. And you tell your children.

Someone was lying on the ground, and people sat about him in a circle. There was a second circle around the first, a third circle, and so on.

Around these circles sat some other people in no particular order.

The man who was sitting in the middle on his side was moving his lips, and everyone around him moved his lips like him.

Then I saw that the man in the middle was no longer there, and all the people sitting about him had stopped moving their lips.

"What is going on?" I asked.

I was told that the man had grown cold and died. Since he had ceased to speak, the others had also ceased to speak.

Afterwards, everyone began running.

I ran after them. I saw two beautiful palaces.

Two ministers were sitting there.

The people ran to the ministers and began to complain to them, "Why did you fool us?" They wanted to kill the ministers. Finally, the ministers ran away.

When I saw the ministers, I liked them very much. I ran after them.

From afar, I saw a beautiful tent.

People shouted from there to the ministers, "Go back! Find all your merits. Take them in your hand and go to the candle that is hanging there. You will be able to accomplish all that you want."

The ministers went back and took their merits. There were bundles of merits. They ran to the candle, and I ran after them.

A lit candle was hanging in the air. The ministers came and threw the merits at the candle, and sparks fell from the candle into their mouths.

The candle turned into a river—the words "the candle" and "river" have the same letters—and everyone drank from it.

Creatures were formed within them. When they opened their mouths to speak, the creatures emerged.

I saw these running back and forth. They were neither human nor animal—just creatures.

Afterwards, the ministers decided to return to their place.

They said, "How can we get back to our place?"

One of them said, "Let us send a message to the person who is standing there, holding a sword from heaven to earth."

They said, "Whom shall we send?"

They decided to send the creatures. The creatures went there, and I ran after them.

I saw a frightening being standing from heaven to earth with a sword in his hand that reached from heaven to earth and had many blades.

One blade was sharp for killing; another was for poverty; another was for weakness. And there were a number of other blades for other punishments.

They began, "It is a long time that we have suffered because of you. Now help us and bring us to our place."

He said, "I cannot help you."

They asked, "Give us the blade of death and we will kill the people."

But he did not agree.

They asked for another blade, but he did not want to give them any blade. So they left.

Meanwhile, an order was given to kill the ministers, and their heads were cut off.

Then things went back to what they had been before.

A person lay on the ground and there were circles of people around him, and they ran to the ministers, and so forth, all over again.

But this time, I saw that the ministers did not throw their merits at the candle. Instead, they took the merits, went to the candle and broke their hearts and began to beg before the candle. Sparks fell from the candle into their mouths.

They pleaded more and the candle turned into a river, and so on, and the creatures were formed. And I was told, "These will live. The first ones were guilty of death because they threw the merits at the candle and did not plead, as these had."

I didn't understand this.

I was told, "Go to a certain room and you will be told what it all means."

I went there, and an old man was sitting there. I asked him what this meant.

He grasped his beard and told me, "This beard is the explanation of the story."

I said, "I still don't understand."

He told me, "Go to such and such a room, and there you will find the explanation."

I went there, and I saw a long, broad, endless room, full of writings. And every place that I opened, I saw an explanation of the story.

Attachment to the Tzaddik

It may be that years pass and you are spiritually stagnant or even regressing. Still, if you are close to a true tzaddik, that alone is of infinite value.

So Far from the Tzaddik

Rabbi Nachman told us that he had had a dream and he didn't know what it meant:

One of my disciples had died (someone who had actually died). But I hadn't known about it until now.

It seemed to me that everyone was standing around me and taking leave of me after Rosh Hashanah, as is the custom.

The man who had died was also standing there. I asked him, "Why weren't you here on Rosh Hashanah?"

He answered, "Hadn't I already died?"

I replied, "Is that a reason? If a man dies, isn't he allowed to come for Rosh Hashanah?"

And the man was silent.

Because a few people were speaking with me about faith in the tzaddik, I also spoke with him about this.

I told him, "Am I the only one in the world? If you don't believe in me, go to other tzaddikim. Since you still believe in others, go to them."

He said, "Whom shall I go to?"

I think that I told him to go to some well-known leader.

He answered, "I am far from him."

I told him, "Go to some other one." I mentioned all the famous leaders. But he said that he was far from every one of them.

I told him, "Since you are far from all of them and you have no one to approach, stay here and grow close to me."

"To you?" he said. "From you I am really very far!"

I believe that it was mid-day, and the sun was directly overhead. The man rose into the air until he reached the sun. He traveled with the sun and they sank bit by bit to the ground together, until he sank below the earth together with the sunset.

He continued with the sun until midnight, when he was directly below me.

Then, when he had sunk so far down, I heard a cry calling to me, "Do you hear how far I am from you?"

And I do not know what this means.

The Prince Who Thought He Was a Turkey

Once there was a prince who thought he was a turkey. He sat naked beneath a table and pecked at bones and crumbs.

All the doctors despaired of healing him, and the king was very sad.

Then a wise man came and said, "I will try to heal him."

The wise man took off his clothes and sat under the table next to the prince, and he also pecked at bones and crumbs.

The prince asked him, "Who are you? What are you doing here?"

The wise man replied, "And what are you doing here?"

"I'm a rooster."

"I'm also a rooster."

The two of them sat there for some time until they grew used to each other.

Then the wise man gave a signal and a shirt was thrown down.

The wise man said to the prince, "Do you think that a rooster can't wear a shirt? One can wear a shirt and still be a rooster."

So both of them put on shirts.

After a while, he gave another signal, and a pair of trousers was thrown down to him.

He said, "Do you think that if someone wears pants, he can't be a rooster?"

This went on until they were both dressed.

Afterwards, he signaled and human food was thrown down from the table. He said to the prince, "Do you think that if you eat good food, you're no longer a turkey? One can eat and still be a turkey." So they both ate.

After that, he told the prince, "Do you think that a turkey can only sit under the table? One can sit at the table and still be a turkey."

And he continued to act in this way until he completely cured the prince.

The Direct Light and the Reflected Light

When you speak with a friend about serving God, your words are a light. Your friend's reaction is a reflection.

Even if your friend doesn't understand you, your light still reflects back from him: you still receive enthusiasm from him. You can be awoken by the reflection of your own words. If you had spoken these words to yourself, they might not have had any effect. But since you spoke them to someone else, you were aroused.

The King and the Bird

Once there was a king who was also an astrologer. He saw that if the wheat was not cut by a certain time, it would get ruined. There was very little time. He decided to hire harvesters and entertain them with all sorts of pleasures and give them everything they needed so that they would be eager to work day and night and cut the grain on time.

But they grew so happy that they forgot. Time passed; they didn't cut the wheat, and it was ruined.

They knew that the king would be angry at them, and they didn't know what to do.

A wise man told them that the king loves a certain bird. The wise man advised them that if they brought the king the bird, he would have so much delight and pleasure in it that he would forgive them everything.

It was very difficult to catch the bird, because it was very high in the air. The people had no ladder, and the time was short.

The wise man advised them that since they are many, they should form a human ladder, one person standing on top of the other, until they reached the bird.

But they fought with each other, because each one wanted to be on top.

Because of their argument they grew careless, and the bird flew away.

As a result, they were left with the king's anger at them for being careless and not cutting the wheat.

It Is Not Good to Be Old

It is not good to be old—not even an old Hasid or an old tzaddik. Being old is not good.

Renew yourself every day; begin at every moment.

The Beggar Who Was Very Old and Very Young

"Here I am," the blind beggar called out to the young, newly-wed couple. "When I came to your wedding, I wished you to be as old as I am. But today I am giving this to you as an outright gift.

"You think that I am blind. I am not blind at all. But to me, all the time of the world isn't worth the blink of an eye."

"I am very old, but I am very young. And I have not even begun to live. Yet I am very old.

"And not only I say this, but I have the testimony of the great eagle.

"I will tell you a story:

Once, people sailed on the sea on many ships. A storm came and wrecked the ships. The people were saved and they went to a tower. When they entered the tower, they found food, drink, clothing and whatever else they needed. They had everything good there, all the pleasures in the world.

They decided that everyone should tell an old story that he recalled from his earliest memory.

There were young and old people there. They asked the oldest person to speak first.

He told them, "What shall I tell you? I remember when the apple was cut from the branch."

No one understood what he meant.

But the wise men who were there said, "Indeed, this is a very old story."

The next-oldest man then spoke. "Is that an old story?" he said. "I remember that, and I also remember when the light was burning."

The people exclaimed, "This is an even older story than the first one!"

They were very surprised that the second man should recall an older story than the first man.

Then they asked the third-oldest man to speak.

He said, "I even remember when the fruit began to form and became a fruit."

The people said, "This story is even older."

Then the fourth-oldest man spoke. "I remember when the seed was planted to form the fruit."

Then the fifth-oldest man said, "I remember the wise men who thought up the seed."

The sixth-oldest man said, "I remember the taste of the fruit before the taste entered the fruit."

The seventh man said, "I remember the fragrance of the fruit before the fragrance entered the fruit."

The eighth man said, "I remember the appearance of the fruit before it entered the fruit."

I was there as well—at that time, I was still a child. I said, "I remember all these things, and I remember nothing."

The people said, "This is really an old story, the oldest of them all."

They were very surprised that this child remembers more than anyone else.

Meanwhile, the great eagle came and knocked at the tower.

He told the people, "Stop being poor. Return to your riches! Use your wealth!" He promised them that they would leave the tower in order of age, the oldest leaving first.

He took everyone out of the tower.

He first called me out, because I was really the oldest of them all. He took the youngest ones out first, and he took out the oldest man last; for whoever was younger was older.

The oldest man was the youngest of them all.

The great eagle said, "I will explain to you all of the stories that everyone told.

"One person told that he remembers when the apple was cut from the branch. He means that he even remembers when his umbilical cord was cut.

"The next man, who told that he remembers when the light was burning, means that he remembers when he was not yet born and a light shone over his head, for the Talmud tells that when a child is in its mother's womb, a light shines over its head.

"The man who told that he remembers when the fruit began to form means that he remembers when his body began to form.

"The man who remembers when the seed was brought to plant the fruit means that he remembers how the drop of semen was drawn down.

"The man who remembers the wise men who thought up the seed meant that he remembers when the drop of semen was still in the mind.

"The man who remembers the taste—that is the nefesh, the lowest level of the soul.

"He who remembers the fragrance—that is the ruach, the middle level of the soul.

"And the appearance—that is the neshamah, the soul's upper level.

"The child who said that he remembers nothing is greater than all of them. He even remembers what existed before these three levels of the soul.

"That is why he said that he remembers nothing—he remembers when nothing existed, which is the very highest level."

The great eagle told the people, "Go back to your ships. They are your bodies that were broken. They will be rebuilt. Today, go back to them."

And he blessed them.

And to me, the blind beggar, he said, "You come with me, because you are like me. Like me, you are very old and very young. You have not even begun to live, but you are very old. And I am the same, for I too am very old and very young."

So I have the testimony of the great eagle that I am both very old and very young, and everything else that I mentioned.

Today I give you an outright wedding gift that you should be as old as I."

There was great joy, and they were very happy.

8. PRAYER

With Prayer, You Can Attain Everything

With prayer, you can attain everything: Torah, serving God, all levels of holiness, and all the goodness in the world.

If a dead person were allowed to return to this world, you can be sure that he would pray with all his might.

What is Hitbodedut?

Hitbodedut is very great. It is higher than everything else.

Practice hitbodedut as follows: set aside at least an hour to be alone in a room or a field, and speak to God in your own words: plead with Him, ask sweetly to be accepted and forgiven—beseech Him to draw you close to Him.

Tell God everything that is in your heart: an expression of regret for the past, a request to come close to Him from this day on, and anything else, according to whatever you are dealing with in your life.

Do this every day for an hour.

And for the rest of the day, be joyous.

This practice is on an extremely high level. It is a very good path and can lead you close to God. It includes everything else. Whatever your imperfections, even if you are completely cut off from serving God, you can speak to Him.

Even if you are so blocked that you cannot say anything, the very fact that you have prepared yourself to stand before God and that you desire to speak is very good.

You can even turn this into a prayer. Cry out to God that you are so far from Him that you find it impossible to speak. Ask Him for compassion to open your mouth.

Many great tzaddikim reported that they only attained their level as a result of this.

The wise person will understand the greatness of this practice, which rises to the very heights.

Anyone, great or small, can do this and come to a great level.

A New Path

On a highway that everyone knows about, murderers and thieves lie in wait. But when one goes on a new path that is still unknown, they do not know about it.

Written prayers are a highway.

Hitbodedut is a new path, a new prayer that one creates from one's heart.

Therefore, negative forces aren't there to such an extent.

Still, do not neglect the regular prayers.

Hitbodedut and the Messiah

There are certainly kosher Jews who do not practice hitbodedut. But I call them confused.

When the Messiah will suddenly come and call them, they will be stunned.

But we will be like a person waking up with a calm mind. Our minds will be clear and undisturbed.

Self-Nullification

Hitbodedut is best done at night, when the world is resting from its labors. During the day, when people are running after this-worldly things, the world keeps a person from clinging to God. Even if one isn't taken up with the vanities of this world, since everyone else is running after them, it is hard to attain self-nullification.

Also, hitbodedut should be practiced in a special place—ideally, outside the city in a lone, unfrequented area. A place that people frequent during the day, chasing after the things of this world, confuses one's hitbodedut even though they aren't there at present, and one cannot nullify oneself to God.

Engage in a great deal of hitbodedut until you nullify one unrefined trait. Then again engage in a great deal of hitbodedut until you nullify another unrefined trait. Continue in this way for a long time until you nullify everything.

If anything is left over, nullify that until nothing remains.

When you come to true self-nullification, your soul is absorbed into its source, God, Who is the necessary existent. Then the entire world is absorbed with your soul into its source. As a result, the entire world becomes a necessary existent.

The Power of Speech

Speech has great power. One can whisper to a rifle to keep it from shooting. Understand this.

Ideally, one should spend the entire day doing hitbodedut.

Since not everyone can do this, at least spend about an hour on hitbodedut. This too is very good.

But if your heart is strong in serving God and you want to really take on the yoke of serving Him, spend the whole day on hitbodedut.

"Would that a person would pray the entire day" (Berachot 21).

Even One Word is Good

Even if you cannot speak, even if you can only say one word, that too is very good.

If you can say only one word, repeat it over and over. Even if you spend a few days on that word, that too is good. Keep repeating the word until God has pity on you and opens your mouth.

The Spider Web

A soldier once attacked a stronghold. When he came to the gate, it was blocked by a spider web. Could there be any greater foolishness than to turn back because of the web?

The essential thing is speech. Through speech, you can conquer everything. You can win all wars.

Although you can do hitbodedut in your thoughts, the essential thing is to say the words out loud.

Sometimes it is difficult to tell God or tzaddikim what is in your heart. You might be embarrassed; you might lack the necessary holy brazenness. This is foolish. You want to use your speech to conquer a great war: the war against your evil inclination. Now, when you are close to speaking, when you are close to conquering the wall and entering the gates, a small obstacle upsets you. Will you stop speaking?

This obstacle is like a curtain of spider webs.

9. THE POWER OF THE MIND

Thought and Visualization

Thought has great power. You can achieve anything that you concentrate on. For instance, if you concentrate on having money, you will definitely become wealthy. The same holds true for anything else.

Your thought must be so powerful that you could sacrifice yourself with it. For instance, you could consciously decide that you are prepared to die for the sake of sanctifying God's name and actually feel the pain of that death.

Like Water on a Stone

Even if many years pass and it appears that your hitbodedut has not accomplished anything, do not be discouraged.

Your words are actually making an impression. They are like water dropping on a stone. Even though it may appear that the water does not affect the stone, if the water keeps falling regularly, it will finally wear a hole through the stone.

Even if you have a heart of stone and your prayer to God doesn't seem to be making any impression, over the course of years, your words will wear a hole through your heart.

The Groom from the World-to-Come

Rabbi Nachman told that he dreamed that he went to a wedding:

I knew the name of the groom.

I looked around and saw a person from the world-to-come, a dead man. I was surprised and said to myself, "If the others see him, there will be a great commotion." I knew his name as well.

The names of the groom and the dead person weren't earthly names, but spiritual names that hint at certain matters, as holy names do.

Afterwards, the others also saw him.

I said to them, "Isn't he dead?'

They only replied, "Still and all," and they weren't disturbed.

Afterwards, I decided to go to the synagogue, from which I would have a better view of the wedding. I circled around and came to the synagogue. At the wedding canopy, the people sang to the groom, "You are a young man, you are a groom." I knew the tune. It was a lovely melody, a melody of joy.

I looked at the scene from the synagogue. Then I decided that I didn't like that spot either, and I went to my house. When I got there, I found the groom lying on the ground. I woke him up: "Aren't they singing to you so much over there—and yet you are lying here?"

(Afterwards, Rabbi Nachman said that it was extraordinary to him that they were singing to him so much over there while he was lying down here.)

In the dream, it appeared to Rabbi Nachman that the place of the synagogue had a different name and the place where he went to his house had a different name. He said that he still knows the names of the groom and the dead person.

And there were other things that he saw in this dream.

One Can Withstand All Lusts

Your consciousness can withstand all lusts.

"The Holy One, blessed be He, gives wisdom to the wise" (Daniel 2:21).

Even if you are drawn after the lusts of this world and have engaged in transgressions that have polluted and constricted your mind, your remaining clear consciousness can still rise. Even one point of consciousness can withstand the entire world with all its lusts.

Wherever you are, you can be close to God.

Even in the depths of hell, you can come close to Him and serve Him.

There Really Is No Lust at All

There really is no lust at all. Eating and drinking are necessary to maintain the body. One must also have children. A person must do all these things. And so there is no lust at all. There is only one condition: one must act with holiness and purity.

The Castle of Water

On the sixth day, the newly-wed couple was joyful and longed for the beggar without hands.

The beggar entered and said, "Here I am. I came to your wedding"—and he continued, telling them what the other beggar had said. Then he embraced and kissed them. And he told them:

You think that my hands are crippled. This is not so. My hands are strong, but I do not use the power of my hands in this world, because I need that power for something else. And I have a testimony to this effect from the castle of water.

Once, a few of us were sitting together. Everyone boasted of the power of his hands.

One person boasted that his hands are so powerful that when he shoots an arrow, he can pull it back.

I asked him, "What kind of arrow can you pull back?" There are ten types of arrows, depending on the ten types of poisons. If one smears them with one type of poison, the arrow is harmful to a certain degree; if one smears it with another kind of poison, it is even more harmful.

I said, "What kind of arrow can you pull back?"

I also asked him, "Can you pull the arrow back before it hits the person, or even after it has already hit the person?"

He replied, "I can pull back one type of arrow even after it has hit the person."

I said to him, "If you can only pull back one type of arrow, you cannot heal the princess."

Another person boasted that he has so much power in his hands that whenever he takes from someone, he gives to him; he is a charitable man.

I asked him, "What kind of charity do you give?"

He answered, "I give a tenth."

I said, "If that is so, you cannot heal the princess. Because you only give a tenth, you cannot go to where she is. You can only enter one wall that surrounds her, you cannot go in to her."

Then another person boasted about the power of his hands. The leaders—kings, ministers, and the like—need wisdom. "I have so much power in my hands," he said, "that I can give each person wisdom with the support of my hands."

I asked him, "What kind of wisdom can you give?"—for there are ten measures of wisdom.

He answered, "I can give one particular type of wisdom."

I said, "If that is so, you cannot heal the princess, because you cannot know her pulse. There are ten pulses. You can only know one pulse, because you can only give one type of wisdom with your hands."

Then another person boasted that he has so much power in his hands that when a storm wind blows, he can hold it back with his hands. He can grab the wind and hold it back. More than that, he can control and calm the wind.

I asked him, "What kind of wind can you grab? There are ten types of wind."

He answered, "Such-and-such a wind."

I said, "You cannot heal the princess, for you can cannot play the tune for her. There are ten types of melody, and the princess is healed by melody. But you can only play one tune for her."

The people there said to me, "What can you do?"

I answered, "I can do what all of you cannot—that is, the nine parts that each of you cannot do."

Here is the story. Once there was a king who desired a princess. He devised all sorts of stratagems to catch her. Finally, he got hold of her, and she stayed with him.

Once, the king dreamed that the princess rose against him and killed him. When he woke up, he was deeply affected by his dream.

He called all the dream interpreters, and they interpreted it according to its simple meaning: that she would kill him.

The king didn't know what to do.

Should he kill her? He couldn't bear that.

Should he send her away? That would upset bother him very much, for someone else would take her. After he had worked so hard for her, she would be going to someone else. And also, if he let her go and she went to someone else, she would certainly be able to fulfill the dream and kill him.

Should he keep her with him? He was afraid that she would kill him.

So the king didn't know what to do.

Because of the dream, his love diminished bit by bit and dwindled away. And her love for him also diminished, until she grew to hate him.

Then she ran away from him.

The king sent men out to look for her. They reported that she was in the area of the water castle.

There is a castle made of water, which is surrounded by ten walls, one around the other. All ten walls are made of water. The castle grounds are also made of water. The garden, with its trees and fruits, is also made of water. The beauty and uniqueness of that castle cannot be told.

One cannot enter the castle because, since it is all made of water, one will drown.

After the princess ran away, she came to the castle and wandered about it.

When the king was told that she was wandering around the water castle, he went with his army to catch her.

When the princess saw this, she decided to run into the castle; she would rather drown than be caught by the king and have to go back to him. Besides, she may be saved.

When the king saw her run into the water, he ordered her to be shot—and if she would die, so be it. The soldiers shot their arrows, and all ten arrows, which were smeared with ten types of poison, hit her.

The princess ran into the water castle, ¬¬passing through all the gates of the watery walls, and got inside. There were gates in the watery walls, and she went through the gates of all ten walls. Finally she entered the castle, and there she fell down in a faint.

I am able to heal her.

He who does not have all ten types of charity in his hands cannot go through all ten walls of the water castle, for he will drown.

The king and his army chased after the princess, and they were all drowned.

But I can go through all ten walls of the water castle.

The walls of water are the waves of the sea that stand like a wall. The winds hold up the waves of the sea, which are the ten walls.

I can go through all ten walls of the water castle.

And I can pull out all ten types of arrows. I know all ten pulses through the ten fingers. Through each finger, one can know a separate pulse.

And I can heal the princess through all ten types of song, for her healing is through melody.

Therefore, I can heal the princess.

So you see, I have the power in my hands.

Today I give you this as a gift.

There was great joy, and they were very happy.

Free Will

Free will is in your hands. That which you want to do, do. That which you don't want to do, don't do.

Tanning the Hide

You must purify your body the same way a tanner works a hide, turning it inside out. You must work your body completely until you can turn it inside out and see that it is completely clean of all desires and bad traits.

10. MONEY

The Tyranny of Wealth

Some people are immersed in wealth. The more wealth they have, the more worries and depression they have: "In sorrow shall you eat it" (Genesis 3:19).

One needs a great deal of wisdom and understanding to keep money from destroying one's life. One can be saved from this only through holy teachings.

The Spiritual Source of Money

All souls are drawn to money. They not only desire money but even the person who has it. "Those who love the wealthy are many" (Proverbs 14:20).

This is because the soul comes from the supernal plane from which money also comes.

The spiritual level from which money devolves is a holy place.

Afterwards, this influx is corporealized into money.

Do not lust for money—that is contemptible. Rather, long for the place from which money comes.

Wealth is a Wall

Wealth is a wall.

And anger is "an open city without a wall" (Proverbs 28:28).

A "wall" is patience: overcoming anger.

When you receive wealth, you receive a wall that stops your anger.

Sometimes, when you grow angry, you harm your wealth.

When you feel overcome with the desire to lose your temper, know that at that moment, some measure of money is slated to be granted from above, and your evil inclination wants to ruin this.

Protect yourself by guarding yourself from anger. Anger harms your soul, as in the verse, "He tears his soul in his anger" (Job 18:3). When you guard yourself from anger and build the wall of wealth, you build your soul. Then all other souls will desire to be included within your soul.

11. THIS WORLD

A Little Coin Before the Mountain

The world stands before one's eyes and keeps one from seeing the light of the Torah and the tzaddikim, a light that is greater than the world by thousands and tens of thousands of degrees.

But if you turn your eyes, lift your head and gaze beyond the barrier of this world, you will see the great light of the Torah and tzaddikim.

This world is like a little coin before your eyes, blocking a great mountain. You can easily move the coin aside and see the mountain.

The Harvest of Poisoned Wheat

Once, a king told his prime minister, "As an astrologer, I see that whoever eats any of the wheat that grows this year will go mad. Let us think of some solution."

The prime minister replied, "Let us have some of last year's wheat set aside for us so that we will not have to eat the poisoned grain."

The king said, "If we do that, we alone will be sane in an insane world. It will be as though we are insane and the others sane. But on the other hand, there isn't enough old wheat to set aside for everyone. So we too will have to eat the poisoned wheat. But we shall make a mark on our foreheads, so that when we look at each other, we will know that we are mad."

The Purpose of This World

The only point of this world is to come to one's ultimate purpose.

Do not be concerned whether or not you have money. Either way, you will live your life the same.

This world fools us completely. It makes a person think that he is constantly earning. But in the end he has nothing. Most people who work for years have nothing to show for it. Even if someone does accumulate money, it is taken from him.

A man and his money cannot remain together. Either the money is taken from the man, or the man is taken from the money. But one never finds that a person remains together with his money.

Also, where is all the money that has been earned since the creation of the world? For all of creation, people have been making money. And where is it all? The truth is that money is nothing at all.

Do Not Let the World Fool You

Do not let the world fool you. There is no one whom this world brings to a good end. All those who held the entire world in their hands came to a bad end, and they even ruined things for generations to come.

This is because there is no this-worldly reality.

What must one do? One needs mercy from heaven to know what to do.

But a Jew already knows what to do, because he has the Torah.

Hidden in a Fist

The evil inclination is like a person running among people with his hand closed. No one knows what he has. He holds out his hand and asks everyone, "What am I holding?"

Everyone imagines that he is holding what one desires. And everyone runs after him.

Then he opens his hand at last, and there is nothing there.

The desires of this world are like sunbeams shining into a house. People want to grasp them, but they grasp nothing.

12. THE END OF DAYS

The Test of the End of Days

Great disbelief will spread throughout the world.

Fortunate is the person who will strengthen himself with faith in those times.

This warning will not help. There were others, such as Daniel, who foretold that before the coming of the Messiah, many will be tested and refined, that the evil will worsen while the wise will keep their understanding.

Many will have their faith tested. The person who will pass the test and retain his faith will be fortunate and will attain all the good that is destined to come (may it be soon and in our days) about which the prophets and wise men prophesied.

If so, everyone should take care to remain strong in his faith. Since this prediction is already common knowledge, there will be no test.

But it will still be a great test.

Many will do evil. "The wicked will act wickedly" (Daniel 12:10).

I am telling you this for the sake of those few good people who will be strong in their faith. They will have great internal battles. But my words will console and strengthen them, for they will see that someone already predicted this.

Greatness in the End of Days

There will come a time when a simple, kosher person will be as extraordinary as the Baal Shem Tov was in his day.

Calculating the Coming of the Messiah

Every time people say the end has come, it is certain that the Messiah is not coming.

The son of David will only come when people are distracted (Sanhedrin 97a).

He will come and he will not be delayed, speedily and in our days, when no one will be calculating that his time has come. Then he will suddenly arrive.

The Messiah Will Come Suddenly

The messiah will come suddenly. There will be a great cry that he has come. Everyone will throw aside his livelihood. The banker will cast aside his business and the candle-maker will cast aside his wax. "They will cast aside their gods of silver and gold" (Isaiah 2:20).

We Have Already Tasted the Good Wine

Once a great merchant traveled with fine Hungarian wine. His servant and wagon driver told him, "We are traveling with this wine, and we are so worn out. Give us some wine to taste."

He gave them some of the wine.

A while later, the servant happened to be among some wine-drinkers in a small town. The others drank wine and praised it highly, saying that it was Hungarian wine.

The servant said, "Let me try it."

When they gave him some, he said, "This isn't Hungarian wine at all."

They were angry and yelled at him. But he answered, "I know that it isn't Hungarian wine because I have already tasted it." But they didn't pay any attention to him.

In the future, when the messiah will come, one will be able to give others Wolochian or Stravitzer wine and tell them that it is good wine. But our people cannot be fooled, for we have already tasted the good wine.

The Golden Mountain and the Pearl Castle

On the road, I told a story, and whoever heard it had an impulse to repent.

This is the story.

Once upon a time, there was a king.

The king had six sons and one daughter.

He thought very highly of his daughter. He loved her very much and took great delight in her.

Once, when he was together with her, he grew angry at her. The words, "May the Evil One take you away!" flew out of his mouth.

That night, the princess went to her room. The next morning, no one knew where she was.

Her father was filled with anguish, and he went around searching for her. When the king's minister saw the king's anguish, he stood up and asked to be given a servant, a horse and money for expenses. He then set off to search for her.

He searched a great deal and for a very long time, until he found her.

This is the story of his search.

He traveled for a long time through deserts, fields and forests.

When he went through one desert, he saw a side road. He thought, "Since I have been traveling for such a long time in the desert and I haven't been able to find her, I will take that road. Perhaps it will lead to a town."

He traveled for a long while. Finally, he saw a fortress surrounded by many soldiers.

Both the fortress and soldiers surrounding it were very fine.

He was afraid that the soldiers would not let him in. Still, he decided to try.

Leaving the horse behind, he went to the fortress.

The soldiers let him in. No one made a move to stop him. He went everywhere, and no one bothered him.

He entered a palace. He saw the king sitting, wearing his crown, and many soldiers standing about him.

Musicians were playing on instruments, and everything was beautiful.

Neither the king nor anyone else asked him anything.

He saw good food, and so he ate. He went to a corner and lay down to see what would happen next.

The king give an order that the queen be brought, and people went to get her.

As the queen was brought out, there was a commotion and great joy, and the musicians played and sang.

The queen was placed on a throne next to the king.

When the minister saw the queen, he recognized her.

The queen noticed someone lying in a corner. When she looked closer, she recognized him. She stood up from the throne, went over to him and touched him. She asked him, "Do you know who I am?"

"Yes, I know you. You are the princess who disappeared. How do you come to be here?"

"I am here because of those words that flew out of my father's mouth. This is the place of evil."

The minister told the princess that her father was filled with anguish, and that he, the minister, had been searching for her for many years.

He asked her, "How can I rescue you?"

She answered, "You can only rescue me if you find a place to sit for one year. For the entire year, only sit and yearn for me. If you do that, you will be able to free me. When you have time, only yearn, desire and hope to take me out. And you must fast. On the last day of the year, you must fast and not sleep for the entire twenty-four hours."

He went and did this. At the end of the year, on the very last day, he fasted and didn't sleep. Then he got up and set out for the princess. On the way, he saw a tree on which grew beautiful apples. They were so beautiful that he went over and ate from them.

As soon as he ate, he fell into a sleep. He slept for a very long time.

His servant tried to wake him, but he could not. Finally, the minister awoke.

He asked his servant, "Where am I in the world?"

His servant told him the whole story. "You have been sleeping for a very long time. A few years have already passed. In the meantime, I lived by eating these fruits."

The minister was filled with anguish. He went to the fortress and found the princess there.

She poured her heart out to him bitterly and in great sadness. "Because of one day, you lost everything. If you had come on that day, you would have taken me out. I know that not to eat is very hard, and particularly on the last day. Then the evil inclination is very strong.

"Choose a spot again and sit there for a year. This time, on the last day, you may eat. But you may not sleep. And do not drink any wine so that you will not fall asleep, for not sleeping is the most important thing."

He went and did all that she said. On the last day, he set out for her. On the way, he saw a running spring. The spring was colored red and smelled like wine. He asked his servant, "Do you see that? This is a spring, but it is colored red and smells like wine!"

He went and tasted the spring.

He immediately fell down and slept for seventy years.

Many soldiers passed by, followed by their belongings. The servant hid from them. Then a carriage passed by, inside of which sat the princess.

When she passed the minister, she stepped down and sat next to him. She recognized him and tried very hard to wake him up. But he could not get up.

She began to rebuke him: "After so much effort and hard work, after so many years that you ran yourself ragged to rescue me, for the sake of one day you couldn't help me. You spoiled everything!" And she cried bitterly.

She said, "It is a great pity on both of us. I have been here so long, and I cannot get free."

She took her kerchief from her head and wrote on it with her tears. She put it next to him. Then she got up and went back to the carriage, and rode away.

Afterwards, the minister woke up. He asked his servant, "Where am I in the world?"

The servant told him the entire story of all the soldiers who had passed by, of the carriage, and of how the princess had cried over him, and that she had said, "It is a great pity on both of us," and so on.

The minister noticed the kerchief next to him. He asked his servant, "Where is this from?"

His servant answered, "She wrote on it with her tears and left it."

The minister took the kerchief and held it up to the sun.

He began to see the letters. He read her complaint and outcry.

He also read that she was no longer in the fortress. Instead, he should search for a golden mountain with a palace made of pearls. "There you will find me," she wrote.

The minister left his servant behind and went to look for her on his own.

He searched for a few years.

Being an expert in maps, he concluded that there was no golden mountain and palace made of pearls in any populated area. He decided that he would go look for her in the deserts, and he spent many years searching for her there.

One day, he saw an inhumanly tall giant carrying a great tree. One could never find such a tree in a populated area. The giant asked him, "Who are you?"

"I am a man."

The giant was astonished. He said, "I have been in the desert a long time, but I have never seen a man."

The minister told him the entire story of his search for a golden mountain and a palace made of pearls.

The giant answered, "There is no such thing." He discouraged the minister and told him, "You were told nonsense. There isn't any such thing."

The minister began to weep with great feeling. "There is such a thing!" he said. "It must exist somewhere!"

The giant again discouraged him, "You were told nonsense."

But the minister said, "It certainly does exist somewhere."

So the giant told him, "I think this is nonsense. But since you are so stubborn, I will you do a favor. I am in charge of all the animals. I will call the animals that run across the entire world to see if any of them knows about this mountain and palace."

He called all the animals from small to great, and questioned them, and they all answered that they had never seen such a thing.

He told the minister, "You see, you were told nonsense. If you would listen to me, you would go back home. You will certainly not find this, because it doesn't exist."

But the minister grew very stubborn and insisted, "It must exist!"

The giant told him, "I have a brother in the desert who is in charge of all the birds. Maybe they know about this golden mountain and palace made of pearls. Since they fly high in the air, maybe they saw the mountain and palace. Go to him and tell him I sent you."

The minister traveled for a few years and searched until he found another giant, who also carried a great tree. This giant questioned him as the first one had and the minister answered him as he had before, adding that the giant's brother had sent him.

This giant also discouraged the minister, and told him that such a thing doesn't exist.

But the minister replied that such a place definitely does exist.

The giant told him, "I am in charge of all the birds. I will call them. Perhaps they know." He called together all the birds and questioned them all, from small to great.

The birds answered that they didn't know of such a mountain and palace.

The giant told the minister, "You see, it definitely doesn't exist. If you would listen to me, you would go back. It doesn't exist."

But the minister grew stubborn and said, "It certainly does exist."

The giant told him, "Farther on in the desert lives my brother who is in charge of all the winds that blow across the world. Perhaps they know about this."

So the minister traveled and searched for several years, until he found another giant who also carried a great tree. This giant asked him the same questions as before, and the minister answered him and told him the entire story.

This giant also discouraged the minister, but the minister pleaded with him. The giant told him that he would do him a favor and call all the winds and question them. He called all the winds and questioned them, but no one knew of the mountain and the palace.

The giant told the minister, "You see, you were told nonsense."

But the minister began to cry, saying, "I know for sure that it exists."

In the meantime, one more wind arrived. The giant rebuked it: "Why are you so late? I commanded all the winds to come. Why didn't you come together with them?"

The wind replied, "I was late because I had to carry a princess to a golden mountain with a palace made of pearls."

The minister was overjoyed.

The giant asked the wind, "What is expensive there?"

The wind replied, "There, everything is expensive."

The giant said to the minister, "You have been searching a very long time for her, and you have worked very hard. It is possible that now you will have a problem because of money. So I will give you a pot. Whenever you put your hand in the pot, you will take out money." He told the wind to carry the minister there. The storm wind came and carried the minister to the mountain and brought him to the door of the town.

Soldiers were standing there, and they didn't let him into the town. He put his hand into the pot and took out money. He bribed them, and went into the town.

It was a beautiful town. He went to a wealthy man and bought food from him. He saw that he would have to remain there a long time, and he would have to use his wisdom and intelligence to rescue the princess.

Rabbi Nachman did not tell how the minister rescued her.

But in the end, he did free her.

Amen Selah.

13. THE LAND OF ISRAEL

Struggling to Come to the Land of Israel

A person who desires to be a Jew—that is, to rise level by level—can only do so via the land of Israel.

Every Jew—whoever really wants to be a Jew—should travel to the land of Israel. Even if you have many obstacles, break through them all and go there. When you manage to come to the land of Israel, you achieve the essence of victory: you are a warrior.

A person has to undergo many sufferings and obstacles before arriving in the land of Israel.

You must be prepared to suffer and break through many obstacles before arriving—for, as our rabbis taught, the land of Israel is one of three things that were given with suffering.

Some people imagine that they are really yearning to come to the land of Israel—if they could travel in comfort. But this is not a perfect desire. A person who really desires to come to the land of Israel must go even by foot.

My Place is in the Land of Israel

My place is only in the land of Israel. In all my travels, I am only traveling to the land of Israel.

The Quality of the Holy Land

The land of Israel seems like any other country. Its soil has the same appearance as the soil of other countries.

But it is really exceedingly holy, at the apex of holiness. Fortunate is the person who has walked there four cubits.

14. SPIRITUAL EVOLUTION

The Dreidel

The world is like a spinning dreidel.

Everything turns around and changes: from man to angel and angel to man; from head to foot and foot to head; everything is revolving and changing from one thing to the next, from top to bottom and bottom to top.

In truth, everything is in its root one.

There are angels, which are totally separated from physicality. There are heavenly beings that are physical, but very fine. And there is our world, which is complete physical.

Even though each one of these three things has its own place, everything is in its root one.

Therefore, the entire world is a revolving wheel, and everything goes around and changes. Now something is at the top like a head and something else is at the bottom like a foot. Afterwards, the foot becomes a head and the head becomes a foot; man becomes an angel and angel becomes a man.

This world is a turning wheel (Shabbat 151b), a spinning dreidel.

This is why people play with a dreidel on Hanukkah.

Hanukkah commemorates the dedication of the Temple.

The Temple demonstrates the upper level coming down and the lower level rising (see Bava Batra 10b). God rested His presence on the Temple. This is the upper level coming down. The form of the Temple was based on a supernal form. This is the lower level rising up.

This is a dreidel, a turning wheel, where everything is transformed.

It is hard to understand how God, Who is so exalted, and higher than all spirituality, could constrict His presence from the highest heavens into the space of the Temple. Nevertheless, God did place His presence in the Temple.

And it is difficult to understand how a human being, who is so low, could make an impression in the upper worlds, or how the sacrifice of an animal could please God. This is God's will—but how can God have a will?

In truth, however, God placed His presence in the Temple, and the animal sacrifices were pleasing to Him.

This is the upper level coming down and the lower level rising; a turning wheel; a dreidel.

Hanukkah commemorates the dedication of the Temple, where above was below and below was above. This is the dreidel, the revolving wheel, things changing from one state to another.

These transformations are the level of the redemption.

In truth, all is one. In its source, all is one.

The World is Improving

God's way is different than that of man. After a person makes a garment, he cares for it as long as it is new. But as it grows older, it wears away and he doesn't think so much of it.

But when God created the world, it was imperfect. Then step by step, it was rectified and He regarded it more highly.

Then came Abraham, Isaac and Jacob, and afterwards Moses. Step by step, tzaddikim rectify the world. Continuously, the world becomes more precious to God. Finally, the Messiah will come and the world will be perfect.

Spiritual Evolution

A number of follies that people used to believe in, such as human sacrifice, have been eradicated.

But the error of war has not been eradicated.

People use their wisdom to make a weapon that can kill thousands of people at a time. But can there be any greater idiocy than destroying many lives for nothing?

The Ultimate Purpose

Everything has a purpose. That purpose has yet another purpose, and so on: higher and higher.

For instance, the purpose of building a house is so that one will have a place to rest. And the purpose of resting is to have strength to serve God.

The purpose of creation is the delight of the world-to-come.

In the Ultimate Places

Rabbi Nachman told this story on the eve of Yom Kippur, after kaparot.

He was walking in a forest. The forest was large and without end, and he wanted to go back. Someone came to him and told him that it is impossible to come to the end of the forest, because it has no end. All the vessels in the world are made from this forest.

But he showed Rabbi Nachman how to get out of the forest.

Afterwards, Rabbi Nachman came to a river, and he wanted to come to the end of the river. Again, someone came to him and told him that it is impossible to come to the end of the river, because it has no end. All the people in the world drink from the waters of this river.

But he showed Rabbi Nachman how to get to the end of the river.

Then Rabbi Nachman came to a mill that was standing by the river. Again someone came to him and told him that this mill grinds the grain for the entire world.

Then he went back to the forest, and he saw a blacksmith sitting there and working. He was told that that blacksmith made the tools for the entire world.

When Rabbi Nachman told this, he said, "The world tells a story, but I have seen a story."

The Level of the Patriarchs

On Rabbi Nachman's return from the land of Israel, he and his companion traveled on a warship: two Jews alone on a vessel manned by Arabs. It was the custom of Arabs—and especially Arab soldiers—to capture Jews and sell them as slaves in distant lands. Rabbi Nachman was very afraid of this.

He began to think: What would he do if he were taken to some far-away place where no Jews live? Who would know of it?

He fell into great anguish: How would he be able to keep the commandments? Finally, he realized that he could serve God even if it were impossible for him to keep the commandments. He realized the level of service that the patriarchs had experienced before the giving of the Torah. They did keep the commandments, although not in the simple sense. For instance, Jacob kept the commandment of tefillin via the branches that he peeled (Genesis 30:37, Zohar 1:162b). Rabbi Nachman realized how he could keep all the commandments in this way.

As soon as he realized that, God helped him and another ship arrived.

Rising to the Ultimate Level

Every spiritual level and every universe contains the levels of "we will do and we will listen" (Exodus 24:7). And every individual contains these levels as well.

"We will do" is the Torah one understands: those things that are revealed. "We will listen" is prayer: hidden things. "We will listen" is also the Torah one does not understand: the Torah of God.

When one rises from one level to the next, one's "listening" is transformed into "doing," and one attains a new level of "listening."

And so it goes from step to step.

Each universe contains "we will do and we will listen."

That which is on the level of "we will listen" for this world is on the level of "we will do" for the next higher world, and that world has its own higher level of "we will listen."

So it goes from world to world.

One must go from level to level and from world to world until one comes to the primal point of creation, the beginning of Emanation.

The level there of "we will listen" is the true Torah of God. On every other level, the "Torah of God" is only called so by analogy: because it is hidden. One can rise to that level, and make it one's own Torah. But the level of "we will listen" at the beginning of Emanation is truly the Torah of God. There is nothing higher. It is the actual Torah of God.

When one clings to the Infinite One, "we will do" is on the level of the actual Torah of God, and "we will listen" is the level of the actual prayer of God.

Apprehending the Ultimate

The universe that God created contains so many wonderful things—how great are the works of God!

Even in this world God's wonders are great. He created inanimate matter, plants, and so on. Who can fathom His greatness in the nature of this world, not to mention the other worlds?

The Sabbath is the purpose of the creation of heaven and earth.

When the world is transformed into a complete Sabbath, people will apprehend God without any barrier. There will be complete oneness. Everyone will point with his finger, saying, "This is God for Whom we have hoped" (Ta'anit 31a).

This is the purpose for which God created the entire universe.

Everything in the world contains a degree of this purpose. Everything in the world has a beginning and an end. The beginning is the spiritual level from which it came until it took on physical form. The end is the purpose for which it was created.

One must look deeply into the details of creation to be able to recognize the greatness of the Creator in everything, serving Him until one comes to the ultimate Sabbath.

People who have great minds can do this.

But smaller people like us are on a very low level, the level of feet, and we cannot attain such knowledge.

Therefore we must yearn for a leader of the generation, a faithful shepherd, who will have the strength to illumine within us the knowledge of how to come to this goal. This leader must be like Moses, who was able to illumine even the lowest of the low.

This leader can even illumine the feet, which are so far from the mind. The people on the level of feet can then know the ultimate purpose through the acts of God in this physical world.

The Sabbath, the world of souls, is clothed in this low world.

We attain the goal precisely through this low world.

The attainment of the ultimate, the attainment of God, depends upon this low world. All souls must pass through this world in order to attain the ultimate. "The Messiah, son of David, will only come when all souls have passed through a body" (Yevamot 62b). All of us must come to this world in order to attain the ultimate.

Everything in this world is necessary, so that through it one may reach the ultimate.

The Intelligence in Everything

Always gaze at the intelligence that resides within every object, with the intention of connecting yourself to that intelligence. That intelligence will shine for you. Then you will be able to come close to God through the object.

However, it is not easy to see the intelligence within every object. The light of intelligence is overwhelmingly great. One can only gain access to it via the constricting spiritual force called the moon.

The moon has no light of its own. All that the moon has is what it receives from the sun of intelligence.

Then "the light of the moon becomes equal to the light of the sun" (Isaiah 30:26).

You must give power to the moon, which is the royalty of holiness, in order to vanquish the royalty of evil.

And how can you do this? By learning Torah vigorously.

When you learn Torah, you give strength to the royalty of holiness. Then this royalty receives life from wisdom. "The light of the moon becomes equal to the light of the sun."

"When the power of holiness rises, the power of evil falls" (Rashi on Genesis 25:23).

Then, all of your entreaties, whether of God or of man, are accepted.

Your words are infused with grace, and your prayers and entreaties are accepted.

Your intelligence illumines you in all matters.

Your intelligence illumines you even in a place that is entirely dark.

This occurs when you look at the intelligence that lies within every object. Then that intelligence brings you close to God.

Gaze upon the intelligence that is in every object.

Do this by learning Torah.

When you learn Torah forcefully, you empower the royalty of holiness to receive from intelligence.

Grace is formed, and your entreaties are accepted.

Then the grace and importance of Israel is elevated. And all their prayers are accepted.

15. IN TWO WORLDS

Leave a Blessing Behind

When one dies, one's soul rises and clings to its level in the upper worlds.

But it is not the soul's ultimate purpose to cling to the upper worlds. The soul reaches its perfection when, while above, it is also below.

One must leave a blessing behind: a child or a student. That way, one's understanding may remain down here below even as one's soul rises.

One should leave behind a child who, like a student, has received one's wisdom and understanding.

The Tzaddik is On All Levels

The wise person who reaches the transcendental energies, the energy flow from the divine Crown, must be able to grasp heaven and earth.

Some people dwell above in heaven, and some dwell below on earth.

The tzaddik must show those who dwell above that they ultimately know nothing of God.

And he must show those who dwell below that "the world is full of His glory" (Isaiah 6:3).

There are people who dwell in the dust, people who are on the lowest level and who imagine that they are very far from God. The tzaddik must awaken them: "Awake and sing, dwellers in the dust" (Ibid. 26:19). He must make it clear to them that God is with them and they are close to Him. He must strengthen them and raise them from despair, for they are close to God, because the entire world is filled with His glory.

In Two Worlds at Once

On the first day of Hanukkah, 5569 (1798), after the lighting of the Hanukkah menorah, a guest entered the house.

He asked the man who lived there, "How do you support yourself?"

The man answered, "I don't have a regular income. I am supported others."

The guest asked, "What are you learning?" and the man told him.

They talked until they began to speak words that come from the heart.

The man who lived there began to yearn a great deal to know how to arrive at a certain level of holiness.

The guest told him, "I will learn Torah with you."

The man was amazed, and he began to think, "Perhaps this guest isn't a human being at all." But when he saw that the guest was talking with him like a human being, his faith in him as a human being was strengthened.

He immediately began to call the guest Rabbi, and he told him, "First of all, I want to learn how to treat you with the proper respect. But it is difficult for a man of flesh and blood to be completely careful. Please teach me how to treat you with the proper respect."

The guest replied, "I don't have time right now. Another time, I will come and teach this to you. But now I have to leave."

The man said, "Tell me how far I should accompany you."

The guest replied, "Past the door."

The man began to think, "How can I go outside with him? Right now, I'm among others (because there were other people in the house). But should I go out with him alone? Who knows who he really is?" He said aloud, "I'm afraid to go out with you."

The guest replied, "Since I can learn with you, if I wanted to do anything to you even now, who could stop me?"

The man accompanied his guest past the door. The guest immediately grabbed him and they began to fly. The man was cold, so the guest gave him a garment. He told him, "Take this garment, it will be good for you. You will have to eat and drink, and you will sit in your house." And he flew with him.

When the man looked around, he saw that he was in his house. He himself didn't believe that he was in his house. But he saw that he was speaking with people and eating and drinking.

In the middle of that, he saw that he was flying, as before. Then he saw that he was in his house again. Then he was flying. This continued for a long time.

The guest brought him down in a valley between two mountains. He found a book there that was filled with combinations of letters: aleph, zayin, chet, dalet, and so forth. There were illustrations of vessels, and inside the vessels were letters. Also, inside the vessels were the letters referring to those vessels—that is, using those letters, one could make those vessels. The man had a great desire to learn that book.

He looked and saw that he was back in his house. Again he looked and he was in the valley.

He decided to go up the mountain. Perhaps he would find a community there. When he climbed the mountain, he saw a golden tree with golden branches. On the branches hung vessels like those that had been illustrated in the book. Inside these vessels were tools by means of which one could make the vessels.

He wanted to take the vessels. But he couldn't, because they were entangled in the crooked branches.

Meanwhile, he saw that he was back in his house.

He found this extraordinary. How was it that he was one moment here and one moment there?

He wanted to tell this to the people in the house, but how could he tell them such an incredible thing?

Meanwhile, he looked out the window and saw the guest. He began to plead with the guest to come in.

The guest said, "I don't have time, because I am on my way to you."

The man said, "This itself is incredible. I'm here, and what do you mean that you are on your way to me?"

The guest answered, "At the moment you agreed to accompany me past the door, I took your neshamah—the highest level of your soul—and gave it a garment from lower paradise, and I left you your two lower soul levels, nefesh and ruach. When you bring your thought to your neshamah, you are there and you draw down an illumination from there to you here. But when you return here, you are here."

I don't know what world he is from. But he is certainly from a good world.

And the story has still not come to its end.

16. HOLY TIME

The Great Wedding

The Sabbath is like a great wedding. Everyone is rejoicing and dancing.

One person is standing to the side, dressed in clothing that doesn't keep out the cold. He runs up quickly and wants to come in and rejoice.

But one needs great merit even to see the wedding through a little crack.

The Holidays Call Out

God's will is revealed through the holidays. Every holiday declares the fact that everything happens only as a result of His will. Holidays are called "a holy calling" (Lev. 23:7): the holiday declares God's will.

On every holiday, God performed great miracles, the opposite of nature. Through this, His will was revealed: the fact that everything is due to His will and that nature does not make anything necessary.

Barrels of Medicine

Once there was a king whose only son grew so ill that all the doctors despaired of healing him.

One day, a very great physician came, and the king begged him to save his son.

The physician replied, "To be completely honest, it is very unlikely that your son can be saved. But still, there is one thing you can try. But I don't know whether to tell you about it, because it won't be easy."

The king begged the physician to tell him what to do.

The physician said, "Your son is so desperately ill that it is impossible to put even a drop of medicine in his mouth.

"There are some drugs that are so expensive that just a small vial costs tens of thousands. You will need to fill barrels full of these drugs, and then pour full buckets over your son. You understand that these drugs will be wasted. But still, your son's body will be strengthened a little bit. And perhaps while the drugs are pouring over him, a drop will trickle into his mouth. This may possibly heal him."

The king immediately agreed to do this and commanded that the physician's instructions be carried out.

As a result, the king's son was healed.

Because we are so spiritually ill, the tzaddik must pour precious medicine over us, even though it seems that almost all of it goes to waste. Still, a good odor remains. And perhaps, over the course of many days, we will be able to swallow one precious, wondrous drop, and we will have the hope to be completely cured, spiritually and physically.

EPILOGUE

Traveling Words

Sometimes, when I say something to someone, my words don't have an effect. They travel from one person to the next until they finally come to a particular person and enter his heart very deeply. Then they awaken him.

SOURCES

Sources:

Great Things: Sichot Haran 51
Without Eating or Drinking: Sipurei Ma'asiyot, Appendix
Believe in Yourself: Sichot Haran 140
Find the Hidden Good: Likutei Moharan 282
A Spirit of Folly: Likutei Moharan II 7
Bring Forth Goodness: Chayei Moharan II, p. 49, #4
Expertise On All Levels: Likutei Moharan 6:4
Do Not Despair: Sichot Haran 3
All Who Hope: Sichot Haran 120
If You Believe That You Can Break...: Likutei Moharan II 112
The Dance: Chayei Moharan II, p. 70, #134
A Broken Heart: Sichot Haran 231
The Cry from the Heart: Sichot Haran 146
Self-Renewal: Sichot Haran 48
A Dream: Chayei Moharan, p. 42, #11
Simplicity: Sichot Haran 235
Fanaticism: Sichot Haran 51
Step by Step: Sichot Haran 27
Desire God: Sichot Haran 51
Receiving the Torah: Likutei Moharan 123
The Crown of the Messiah: Avaneha Barzel, p. 23
The Simplicity of God: Sichot Haran 101

The Clever Man and the Simple Man: Sipurei Ma'asiyot, The Clever Man and the Simple Man
The Blink of an Eye: Chayei Moharan II, p. 42, #2
It is Forbidden to Despair: Likutei Moharan II 78
The Task of Joy: Likutei Moharan II 24
Accept Everything with Joy: Chayei Moharan, p. 76, #2
The Greatness of Faith: Sichot Haran 33
The World Was Created for Faith: Sichot Haran 222
The Chambers of Torah Insight: Likutei Moharan 245
Yearning to Learn: Likutei Moharan 142
When the Torah Shows its Love: Sichot Haran 17
Discipline and Liberation: Sichot Haran 19
Dozing Off While Learning: Sefer Hamidot, Learning 6
Learn Aloud: Likutei Moharan 118
The Traveler through Torah: Sichot Haran 28
How to Learn Torah: Sichot Haran 76
Success through Visualization: Sichot Haran 62
God Enjoys Your Torah Thoughts: Likutei Eitzot: Talmud Torah 47
Creating Rivers of Torah: Likutei Moharan 262
Creating One's Own Torah Thoughts: Likutei Moharan II 105
Torah Insights: Likutei Moharan 118
Giving God Joy: Sefer Hamidot, Learning 3
Cultivating Torah Insights: Sichot Haran 58
The Protection of Learning Jewish Law: Likutei Moharan II 21
Torah Without Insights: Likutei Moharan 21:8
Clarifying Character Through Halachah: Sichot Haran 29
Guarding One's Mind: Likutei Moharan 35:2
The Map of Time and Space: Sipurei Ma'asiyot, from The Master of Prayer
Even if You Cannot Sing Well, Sing: Sichot Haran 273
The Melody of Faith: Likutei Moharan 64:5
The New Song of the Future: Likutei Moharan II 8:10
Stories Wake People Up: Chayei Moharan, p. 16, #25
Folk Tales and Holy Secrets: Sipurei Ma'asiyot, Introduction
Foolish Things: Chayei Moharan II, p. 72, #141
The Story of the Humble King: Sipurei Ma'asiyot, The Humble King
The Man of Compassion: Likutei Moharan II 7
The Tzaddik is Both Above and Below: Likutei Moharan II 68

The Light That Shines in a Thousand Universes: Sichot Haran 93
The Field of Souls: Likutei Moharan 65:1
Mercy, the Heart and the Spring: Sipurei Ma'asiyot, from The Seven Beggars
The Journey of the Dead Merchant: Chayei Moharan, p. 47, #21
How to Become a Tzaddik: Sichot Haran I 26
Untutored Piety: Sichot Haran 76
The Tzaddik and Trust in God: Sefer Hamidot, Tzaddik 103
Vision of the Man in the Circle: Chayei Moharan, p. 36, #2
Attachment to the Tzaddik: Chayei Moharan II, p. 19, #25
So Far from the Tzaddik: Chayei Moharan p. 46, #21
The Prince Who Thought He Was a Turkey: Kochavei Ohr, p. 26
The Direct Light and the Reflected Light: Likutei Moharan 184
The King and the Bird: Kochavei Ohr, p. 28
It is Not Good to be Old: Sichot Haran 51
The Beggar Who was Very Old and Very Young: Sipurei Ma'asiyot, from The Seven Beggars
With Prayer, You Can Attain Everything: Likutei Moharan II 111
What is Hitbodedut?: Likutei Moharan 2:25
A New Path: Likutei Moharan II 97
Hitbodedut and the Messiah: Sichot Haran 228
Self-Nullification: Likutei Moharan 52
The Power of Speech: Likutei Moharan II 96
Even One Word is Good: Likutei Moharan II 96
The Spider Web: Sichot Haran 232
Thought and Visualization: Likutei Moharan 193
Like Water on a Stone: Sichot Haran 234
The Groom from the World-to-Come: Chayei Moharan, p. 43, #13
One Can Withstand All Lusts: Sichot Haran 51
There Really is No Lust at All: Sichot Haran 51
The Castle of Water: Sipurei Ma'asiyot, from The Seven Beggars
Free Will: Likutei Moharan II 110
Tanning the Hide: Chayei Moharan II, p. 5, #5
The Tyranny of Wealth: Likutei Moharan 23:5
The Spiritual Source of Money: Likutei Moharan 68
Wealth is a Wall: Likutei Moharan 59:5
A Little Coin Before the Mountain: Likutei Moharan II 119

The Harvest of Poisoned Wheat: Avaneha Barzel, p. 27
The Purpose of This World: Sichot Haran 51
Don't Let the World Fool You: Sichot Haran 51
Hidden in a Fist: Sichot Haran 6
The Test of the End of Days: Sichot Haran 35
Greatness in the End of Days: Sichot Haran 36
Calculating the Coming of the Messiah: Chayei Moharan II, p. 61, #81
The Messiah Will Come Suddenly: Chayei Moharan II, p. 74, #145
We Have Already Tasted the Good Wine: Chayei Moharan II, p. 10, #20
The Golden Mountain and the Pearl Castle: Sipurei Ma'asiyot, The Lost Princess
Struggling to Come to the Land of Israel: Chayei Moharan p. 12, #15
My Place is in the Land of Israel: Chayei Moharan, p. 68, #6
The Quality of the Holy Land: Likutei Moharan II, 116
The Dreidel: Sichot Haran 40
The World is Improving: Sichot Haran 239
Spiritual Evolution: Chayei Moharan II, p. 64, #99
The Ultimate Purpose: Likutei Moharan 18
In the Ultimate Places: Chayei Moharan, p. 44, #15
The Level of the Patriarchs: Shivchei Haran 23
Rising to the Ultimate Level: Likutei Moharan 22
Apprehending the Ultimate: Likutei Moharan II 39
The Intelligence in Everything: Likutei Moharan 1
Leave a Blessing Behind: Likutei Moharan II 7:4
The Tzaddik is on All Levels: Likutei Moharan II 7:7
In Two Worlds at Once: Chayei Moharan, p. 39, #5
The Great Wedding: Sichot Haran 254
The Holidays Call Out: Likutei Moharan II 4
Barrels of Medicine: Chayei Moharan II, p. 32, #51
Traveling Words: Sichot Haran 208

ABOUT THE TRANSLATOR

Yaacov David Shulman has authored and translated fifty books dealing with Jewish spirituality, such as the works of Rabbi Nachman of Breslov, Rav Avraham Yitzchak Kook, Rabbi Kalonymus Kalman Shapira, and others. He has also written books of poetry.

Find out more at ydshulman.com and ravkook.net.

To contact the translator: yacovdavid@gmail.com.

www.ingramcontent.com/pod-product-compliance
Ingram Content Group UK Ltd.
Pitfield, Milton Keynes, MK11 3LW, UK
UKHW022013190726
13853UKWH00005B/1906

9 798793 604826